Romance Da

ROMANCE DAWN

**First edition. November 18, 2023.**



ISBN: 979-8223686057

Written by Sakari Lacross.

# Table of Contents

# Infinite Dream

I'm up at night

Thinking about our romance

This Saturday night

Turning over, from Friday.

I'm in a bed for two

And it's only me

Rocking myself to sleep

Your head, against my chest

Where will I place these memories

Once they finally reach me

~ *Sakari*

All you can love

You tell me, to take the lead

I've been single, for so long

On top of you, you're pulling me.

And as our legs, our ankles, and our feet touch

Our stomachs, our chests, and our lips touch.

Our hands, our feelings, and ourselves, we touch

Our weekends, our nights, and our seasons touch.

~ *Sakari*

I'm scared of you

Feelings that break out for you

I'm scared of you

Being in touch, with all of you

~ *Sakari*

Please, please, please, please

Treat me, like you say

Please, please, please, please

Love me, while we're not over

~ *Sakari*

I don't need to wonder anymore

That's the beauty of it

Bleached my worries away

You're the beauty from this

~ *Sakari*

I feel like, I'd marry you.

Complete more than, a sentence with you.

Have more than, two kids with you.

Spend more than, time with you.

*~ Sakari*

Gone past the clouds

I'm taking you

Love in the dark, with sound

Your lips hum

All around a room

We're taking

Things into reverse

But you're always naked

~ *Sakari*

I won't let Autmn past

I'm loving you

Right through cuddle season

We'll change with the leaves

*~ Sakari*

Take me wherever you are

Two different Infinites

A sky, that finally meets...

The ground.

Air that feels looser

Than usual

This domain

You've brought me to...

~ *Sakari*

# Astral Plane

I wanna be the one

To wait for your love

The most patient of one

The one who shows

That the sands may drag me...

The winter may try...

But on this course, I remain...

I go nowhere, waiting...

For you and I...

~ *Sakari*

More poetic

Than a landscape

This falling, I disappear

Faster, in your valley

Your body has values

When I see it, for myself

I deep dive

From your cliff

Into you...

*~ Sakari*

You can see our love

Just as much as I can

Neither of us are in trouble

I can wait, as long as you can

*~ Sakari*

Deeply rooted

We'll keep this tree of ours

Alive.

And it'll grow us

A better future

Alone, we'll never be.

So the dragon between us

Can be defeated

The final chapter

Awaits us...

*~ Sakari*

There's no guide

Though I know where we are

I'll find you

Purely off, following my heart

~ *Sakari*

Your sea will part

I...will drown.

Your waves will ravage me

I...will drown.

*~ Sakari*

Through your portal

I find a garden

It's only me

And trees

All nature.

It's only me

There's light but no sun

A linear place

There's only one way to go

Off in the distance.

*~ Sakari*

Words have never been so untrue

You deserve, all that is shown to you.

When your eyes close, and you cry in your sleep

That happiness you see, is meant for you

~ *Sakari*

Taking you in, like it's yesterday

In my mind, we're on your couch.

And I dreamed of this, yesterday

You in that black getup, on the couch.

From the selfie you sent me

I envy

The guys in Cali

That pass by you

So treat me like any Wednesday

And let me, pass by you

Taking you in

Like yesterday

~ *Sakari*

# Enjoying The Time I Know You

This is something

We do in person

In person, our love

Will be better.

My first Scorpio

It's an illusion

This distance

Doesn't stop us.

~ *Sakari*

I woke up, and didn't see you

Next to me

When did I go to sleep?

You text me, telling me

You had a dream

I was in it.

What did we do, baby?

What about it, did you love, baby?

*~ Sakari*

In my new apartment

I'd bring you

I can't wait until November

Watch me, bring you...

The moonlight on your back

Where did heaven drop you off at?

I'm so in love, you didn't even

Take your clothes off, yet

Bring tonight, into tomorrow.

Please stay with me

I won't let you cry over me

My mentality, tells on me

I'm easy going...

In my new apartment

I'd bring you

I can't wait until November

Watch me, bring you...

The moonlight on your back

Where did heaven drop you off at?

I'm so in love, you didn't even

Take your clothes off, yet

*~ Sakari*

I'm gonna take your love with me, to Infinity

That night...

~ *Sakari*

You'd come this way, for me

I'm used to girls getting their way

And doing nothing

For me.

Girls who never really

Wanted me

Girls that aren't like you

You want me.

*~ Sakari*

Pick my heart up

It's lighter than you believe

My heart now levitates

To your touch

A float of love

Air driven, because of you

~ *Sakari*

There must be a reason

You're holding on

Perfect lady, why me?

You told me to stop asking

"Why me"

Believing that you're

The average human being...

~ *Sakari*

Between sweets and a cake

Our love was made

Promises by candles

We blow them out

Easily

I'm in love with you

~ *Sakari*

But I don't wanna...

She tells me to go ahead.

I try not to....

But she holds me in.

All of me

Now bottled within her...

Liquids from me

Stored inside of her....

*~ Sakari*

# Without A Curse

I swear I've lived this universe without you

And I swear, I used to hate it

~ *Sakari*

I would never ask you for nudes

Never ask you to send parts of yourself

Through a message.

Never will I ask you to prove your beauty

Without clothes

I know you're beautiful...

~ *Sakari*

All I've ever wanted to be

Is important to you.

That's all I've ever wanted

No strings attached...

*~ Sakari*

You say I'm beautiful

But my personality is wretched

Why can't I commit

Like you?

~ *Sakari*

# Up Close & Ready

Don't sleep without my arm around you

Don't sleep with doubts on your heart

Don't sleep with your makeup smeared

Don't you fall asleep, beautiful...

~ *Sakari*

I'm sorry for this obsession

I feel obligated

To ensure...

I'm sorry for not giving you

What I wanted to meet you with

Wealth and love, at the same time.

~ *Sakari*

I'm not trying enough

You're not gaining from me

Enough.

You look like an "Only Fans"

How did I get you

Through a message?

~ *Sakari*

Low on your body

I can't get much lower

Without being in love.

My mouth against

Your chance maker

I'm in love.

*~ Sakari*

All raw and pure

Emotions on the inside

I can feel them.

I can feel your moans

When you say you love me

I can feel you...

~ *Sakari*

I never asked you

If you preferred

Fast or slow?

Strong or careful?

Top or bottom?

Kisses to the lip, or the neck?

~ *Sakari*

I'm my mind we're forbidden

You tell me, that's not reality

~ *Sakari*

# Overly Dedicated

My love,

I'm going to do everything in my power

To get to u.

I love u too much

Not to get to u.

Just accept me, babe

When I'm finally around you.

~ *Sakari*

I'm getting on my knees for you

I'm licking your lips, while you stand on your feet.

I'm getting on my knees for you

Asking you, if there is anyone else, you'd ever consider.

I'm getting on my knees, my love

Speaking to you, like I'm not worthy

I'm getting on my knees, my Goddess

Begging you to grant me, access to your fountain.

*~ Sakari*

You can do whatever to me

Do whatever with me

You've got me by the strings, girl.

Even though you call me your king

Even though you tell me to take lead

You swear you're following me

But I'm only, here for you...

I wanna touch your skin

Put your hair in my hands

Spank you like you're wrong.

Tug on your pink thong

Nibble on your belly button piercing

Please you in the shower

Drink from your water...

~ *Sakari*

Bouncing on top of me

I can't wait to see

Your body perform.

I'm not predicting a thing

I'm going in blind

Uncovering the secrets, in your panties

~ *Sakari*

Black chains around my neck

Black chains, black chains...

If it's you that I'm now seeing

Can I see, can I see...

Show me something, before hand

Use me, before hand

Traces along your panties, before hand

I can't wait to lick on you, before hand

~ *Sakari*

Need me, for a minute

Cherish me, for an hour

Own me, afterwards

Or give me permission to own you

In an hour...

*~ Sakari*

Someone's losing you

And it isn't me this time

I'm losing myself

But at least it isn't you, this time

~ *Sakari*

For someone as alluring as you

Why don't you make me

Chase the stars...

*~ Sakari*

The sky came down to me

When you decided to go out your way

And talk to me

~ *Sakari*

# Alone @ 11pm

All I do is convince myself

That I'm the one for you

All I do...

All I do is pray for your love

Given that we're always together, in some way

All I do...

Is run after you, during a dreamscape

Your beautiful essence, in this dream domain

All I do...

~ *Sakari*

I'm starting to dream

About having a family with you

You tell me three

I tell you, "by when?"

~ *Sakari*

I hate the nighttime

Because I know

You take an early bedtime.

U unwind

Put your evening's time

On your son

With dinner's time

Taking up more time.

~ *Sakari*

Make me feel worth it

In the end

Because with one kiss

All my doubts, could end

~ *Sakari*

You're a dream to me

I want to catch you

Before I wake up

~ *Sakari*

Do you have a minute?

Somethings been going on, and...

Would you come with me?

See if anything is there.

Or am I being a nuisance

At this point.

~ *Sakari*

Thank you

For making me a choice.

For having me.

For doing for me.

I can barely, do for myself.

Thank you

This doesn't feel real.

Why would you do this, for me?

Why would you call me, your king?

I can barely, do for myself.

~ *Sakari*

# I'm Not Leaving You

And I keep feeling like crap

Because I'm in love with you

But I have nothing to show for you

I'm a stage without a show

~ *Sakari*

In your jeep, can we go

To your backseat?

Am I worthy

Of seeing you spotless?

~ *Sakari*

You're sporting everything you wear

Hug yourself for me

The snow here has melted for me

Though I'm still cold, without you here

*~ Sakari*

You've edited my heart

From all these grammars

You're no editor

But my purpose, is looking better

~ *Sakari*

Don't start your day without me

I'm behind you, with engine in chest

~ *Sakari*

Making up and making love

Making us and making memories

Making plans into reality

Making you feel less and less alone

~ *Sakari*

You've got me worried

Taking in your form of love

In the form of 30's

I've never had, a Scorpio before.

A few things don't matter

How does how we fell in love

Really matter?

I'm on your love, I took a 30

October 31st, you're almost 30

So baby, it's 30

I've got 30 forms of life

To give you.

~ *Sakari*

Koveli

I can't wait to meet you

To treat you like you're mine

To never abandon you, baby boy.

Placing a title on me

Only your mother can do that

But Koveli, I wanna raise you

As if you were my own.

*~ Sakari*

I think it's so sexy

How you haven't spoken to anyone else

Since your heart has been broken.

So sexy

That you haven't had favorites

Since your first love

Even more sexy

That you've fallen again

And it's with me

~ *Sakari*

Of course, you're so beautiful

I just wanna kiss you

And be kind to you

All the way

*~ Sakari*

We're in space.

No.

We're in infinity.

No!

We're in love.

It just feels like those things.

~ *Sakari*

I'm human again.

I'm emotional and embarrassed

Again.

I lack a thick layer of skin

Again.

I'll never change

Again.

~ *Sakari*

You've cried twice

In the same night

I would never allow

Something like that to happen

~ *Sakari*

I'm hanging off a cliff

In my mind

You grab my hand

To save me

Let go, Angelina

I'd never put you in danger

*~ Sakari*

If you were kissed properly

Your lips still wouldn't feel

This ashamed

~ *Sakari*

I never thought about anything first

I just dove in after you

Knowing that time was running out

For the both of us

~ *Sakari*

Don't you feel it?

I will never leave you

For someone I used to love.

I still love you

So there is nothing she can do.

~ *Sakari*

I pray nothing happens

Before I get to you.

Nothing happens

Before we complete each other.

Nothing happens

Before I reach you

Nothing happens

Before I adore you, in person

~ *Sakari*

I'm thinking about Cali's eve

We're warming up, before it starts to freeze

I'm on both knees.

You're laying on the edge of the bed

Your legs spread, hands behind my head

Moisture blocking, anything that could be said.

Nails done and perfect

A four day trip to you

That tastes, so worth it

~ *Sakari*

Just message me baby

You don't have to call me.

Keep my focus

Away from all the demons

That are behind me

*~ Sakari*

Some sort of infinity

Caught between two galaxies

You are...

A rift in a dimension

That cheats its way

To Heaven...

~ *Sakari*

## Don't miss out!

Visit the website below and you can sign up to receive emails whenever Sakari Lacross publishes a new book. There's no charge and no obligation.

https://books2read.com/r/B-A-GXQL-AAWQC

BOOKS 2 READ

Connecting independent readers to independent writers.

# Also by Sakari Lacross

**A Dawn Breaking Romance**
Romance Dawn

**Endless Journal**
Wherever You Might Be
Something Else To Hurt About
Something Else Entirely
I Once Had A Heart
Mood
Another Mood
Patient Hearts
Never Ending
Unspoken Words
The Realm In Between

**Eternal Flames**
Burn Brothers

**Lyrics**

Lyrics

**Mental Health**

PTSD

Anxiety

Schizophrenic

**My Soul Mate**

The Only Girl I Really Want

**Perfect Gentleman**

Perfect Gentleman

**Sunset Szn**

Sunset Szn

Sunset SZN 2

Sunset SZN 3

**This Is For Her**

Someone Like You

Someone Like You Too

Someone Else Like You

**Standalone**

The Legend Of Krampus

# About the Author

Michael Wayne Noland Jr, better known for his pen name Sakari Lacross, was born February 5th, 1994 in Cleveland Ohio. Spending most of his childhood being raised in Flint Michigan, Michael's mother moved him and his family to Arizona when he was 15. Even with his unstable background, Michael has been writing since he was nine years old, competing in his school's poetry contest and bimonthly writing events. Discovering all his true potential to write during his years he went to linden charter academy, Michael won his first local poetry contest at Sam Garcia Western Avenue Library, located in Avondale Arizona. Michael then published his first poetry collection, titled, PTSD. With so many more projects on the way, Michael has no plans of stopping his love for writing any time soon and encourages his readers to stick around for the rides to come.

Milton Keynes UK
Ingram Content Group UK Ltd.
UKHW020625291123
433416UK00016B/1050

9 798223 686057